HOCKEY CANADA

DOMINANT
DANY HEATLEY

DANY HEATLEY

WITH
LORNA SCHULTZ NICHOLSON

Fenn Publishing Company Ltd.
Bolton, Canada

Fenn Publishing Company Ltd.

DOMINANT DANY HEATLEY

A Fenn Publishing Book / First Published in 2008

We acknowledge the financial support of the Government of Canada through the Book Publishing Industry Development Program (BPIDP) for our publishing activities This book is licensed by Hockey Canada.

Hockey Canada and the Hockey Canada logo are registered trademarks and may not be reproduced without the prior written consent of Hockey Canada.

Designed by First Image
Fenn Publishing Company Ltd.
Bolton, Ontario, Canada
Printed in Canada

Library and Archives Canada Cataloguing in Publication

Heatley, Dany
Dominant Dany Heatley / Dany Heatley and Lorna Nicholson.
ISBN 978-1-55168-344-7

1. Heatley, Dany. 2. National Hockey League--Biography.
3. Hockey players--Canada--Biography. I. Schultz Nicholson, Lorna II. Title.

GV848.5.B76B34 2008   796.962092   C2008-902089-8

DOMINANT DANY HEATLEY

CONTENTS

Foreword 4

Silver Lining 6

From Germany to Canada 10

Big Decision, Big Payoff 20

The Big Leagues 30

Trophies and Medals 40

Twists and Turns 50

Ottawa and the Olympics 68

Stanley Cup Finals 74

Acknowledgements/Photo Credits 80

FOREWORD

At the start of each new NHL season, I am always interested in the new young rookie talent. I often wonder, as I watch them play, if they will stick with this game that I love so much, or leave the league after only a short stint. Some players come and go, while others remain in the game for the long haul. That's just how it is.

When I first heard about Dany Heatley, I was told he was someone to watch. I was impressed when I saw first-hand just how good he was at the 2002/2003 season All-Star game. He was part of the Eastern Conference Team and by the end of the second period he had scored four goals. He had tied the record that I shared with Vincent Damphouse, Mike Gartner and my good friend, Mario Lemieux. During the flood between second and third periods, I went down to see Dany to congratulate him on his performance. I'd never really met him before. In all honesty, I would have loved to see him break the record and score another goal in the third period. When a young kid breaks a record it keeps the game of hockey alive. Everyone talks and writes about it. Dany was good in that third period but never found the net for that fifth goal, though he did break my record for youngest player to score four goals in an All-Star game!

Over the years, I have had the honour of working with Dany on Team Canada and I have been really impressed with the way he carries himself on and off the ice.

When Dany went through his tough times off the ice, I wondered if he would stick with hockey. I understand how tough it is to be in the public eye for something other than your hockey and it would have been easy for him to disappear from the game. But Dany remained a passionate, hard working hockey player and I really admire him for that. His actions and dedication tell me that he plays hockey for the love of the game. And to me that means a lot.

I hope you enjoy reading about Dany Heatley as much as I have enjoyed watching him play hockey over the years.

Wayne Gretzky

SILVER LINING

The 2008 IIHF Men's Worlds were held for the first time in Canada.
Team Canada had a great series, except for our last game.

I am a true Canadian hockey player and none of us like the silver medal. We are not satisfied winning anything less than gold for our country. When I was asked to play for Canada in the 2008 International Ice Hockey Federation (IIHF) World Championships I said yes immediately. It was a big deal because for the first time in the Federation's 100–year history, the event was being held in Canada. My season with the Ottawa Senators was over and like my teammates I was still upset about losing to Pittsburgh in the first round. We had an amazing start to the 2007/08 NHL season and had tied the NHL record for the fastest team to have 15 wins, which we achieved by November 15, 2007 after just 17 games. Then after Christmas we just couldn't seem to get our winning streak back.

We were up and down and couldn't find consistent play. Losing to Pittsburgh in four games in the first round of the playoffs was not fun. But then I got the call to play for Team Canada and I was ready to put my skates on again. The World Championship team that Hockey Canada assembled was great. We played our preliminary games, qualification games and our quarter-final game all in Halifax, Nova Scotia. Our coach Ken Hitchcock put me on a line with Rick Nash and Ryan Getzlaf and we really clicked. It was fun to be back scoring goals.

We won each of our qualification games. Then after beating Norway in the quarter-final game we boarded a chartered flight and headed to Quebec. We were undefeated and so was Russia. We beat Sweden in the semi-finals and Russia bettered the Finns, setting the scene for a Russia-Canada gold-medal contest. I headed into the gold medal game tied with Eric Lindros for most goals in this tournament. Lindros scored 11 goals in 1993. At this point I had 11 goals and 8 assists. I wanted to score and break the record of course, but more than that, I wanted my team to win the gold medal.

We started off great in the gold medal game. The Russians scored first but then Brent Burns scored for us to tie the game at a goal a piece. Brent scored again, followed by a goal by Chris Kunitz and when the buzzer sounded the end of the first period, Canada was up 3-1. I hadn't scored yet so Lindros' record remained intact. During the intermission, I got myself pumped to just keep shooting. The Russians scored fairly quickly into the second period to make the score 3-2. That gave us a bit of a scare as anything can happen in a one-goal game.

When I scored Canada's fourth goal, I was ecstatic. It was my 12th goal of the tournament and I had broken the all-time scoring record in the modern era! I honestly thought at that moment that we had the game in the bag. We were still up 4-2 going into the third and with just eight minutes left in the third period we were still ahead by two goals. We were playing a bit on our heels, however, and not winning the faceoffs. Then the Russians scored to make it 4-3. We fought to hold on but the Russians scored again to tie the game and force overtime. Just two minutes into overtime, we took a penalty. The puck got away from Rick Nash and he shot it over the boards. It was definitely a questionable penalty but the referee ruled it anyway. Rick had been having such a great tournament and he was totally choked about the call.

It was a sick feeling when Russia scored during that penalty. I hate losing. All of my teammates felt the same and the dressing room after that game was so unbelievably quiet. I thought about the loss all night and it made my stomach sick. Canadian hockey players hate finishing a tournament with anything but a gold medal.

I guess the only silver lining, for me personally, was that I won the MVP of the tournament and I broke the scoring record. My goal also gave me 20 points, which tied me with Steve Yzerman's 1990 Canadian points record, though I can honestly say that I would have traded the record for Canada to win gold!

I now look forward to the 2010 Olympics with determination— to play for Canada and get that gold medal back. And I'm looking forward to the 2008/2009 season with the Ottawa Senators and going further than the first round in the playoffs.

I'm still young and I have a lot more years to play the great game of hockey.

I hope you enjoy my story.

I won player of the game for Canada in our game against Slovenia. I also won MVP for the entire tournament.

FROM GERMANY TO CANADA

CHAPTER ONE

Although I was born in Germany, I do have some real Canadian hockey in my blood. My father, Murray Heatley, grew up playing minor hockey in Calgary, Alberta and then went on to play professional hockey. The year I was born he scored 68 goals for his pro team in Europe. My father played in Freiburg, Germany in the European Hockey League and everyone tells me he was a fast-skating winger. I am proud of that.

I am often questioned about the spelling of my name and asked if I've forgotten to write the second 'n,' well in Germany, Dany is spelt with just one 'n', opposed to with two n's as common in North American spelling.

I was born on January 21, 1981, in Freiburg. Although my official name is Daniel, I like Dany much better. While I have both Canadian and German citizenship, I play international hockey for Canada. I feel it's a real honour to play for Canada.

Before I was born my dad had a long and varied hockey career. He attended the University of Wisconsin, in Madison, on a hockey scholarship. In his four years with the Wisconsin Badgers, he earned three letters because he played on the varsity team for three years and for each year he received a letter. He also scored many goals. Once he graduated from the University of Wisconsin, he signed with the Toronto Maple Leafs and played in the minors until he was traded to Vancouver. Three months after his trade, he decided to jump from the NHL to the WHA (World Hockey Association), where he played seven seasons before deciding to play in Europe.

When he made his decision to play hockey in Europe, he didn't realize that it would change his entire life. He didn't know that he would meet my mom, get married and start a family.

I feel pretty lucky that hockey was in my blood before I was even born, though my mom tells me that it came exclusively from my dad. A few years before I was born, my dad met a girl

◄ *I loved playing baseball when I was a kid. I think it's good for all young hockey players to play other sports.*

in Germany named Karin Slawinski. (My dad always says she was the prettiest girl in Germany.) My mom was from Berlin, Germany and they met through mutual friends.

When my mom and dad met, she had never seen a hockey game! Ever. Can you believe that?

That must have been hard for my dad to understand. Everyone in Canada has seen at least some sort of hockey game. My mom was twenty years old. She started attending my dad's hockey games and learned that she liked the speed of the game. Just one year later my mom and dad were married. They decided to have two weddings. The first was held in Calgary because that is where my dad's family lived, followed by a second saying of the vows at a traditional German wedding in Frieburg, Germany, with my mom's family.

My mom and dad chose to live in Germany after they were married. I was their first son. My mom talks about when I was little all the time and she likes to tell me—and everyone else who will listen—about how I couldn't sit still. Sometimes she just looks at me and says, "You were always moving. And you had a strong will. I couldn't hold you back." My mom is great! She makes me laugh.

I got my first hockey outfit at the age of two—but it was a referee's outfit!

You know what my mom tells people? "Dany got that outfit for Christmas. He loved to wear it and he would put it on and walk around with a hockey stick in one hand and a ball in another."

Me, in a referee's outfit? That is so crazy. My dad always says that he knew I wouldn't end up a referee.

My parents lived in a small apartment in Germany and there wasn't much room for me to play hockey. My mom put together a scrapbook of our time in Germany and there is this old photo in it of me when I was around two years old. I have the laundry hamper over on its side so I could use it as a goalie net. My mom said I did that because there was no room in the apartment for a real hockey net.

Here's me with the laundry hamper upside down so I could use it as my goalie net. My dad is in the background feeding my baby brother, Mark.

My first jersey was striped! My mom tells me that I loved that jersey.

When I was three, my dad chose to end his hockey career. My parents then had a big decision to make—stay in Germany or move to Canada. After many long talks, they knew that if they wanted more land and a bigger house they would have to move to Canada. They also knew that it would be far easier for my dad to get work in Canada.

Sadly, my mom packed all the family belongings and moved away from her homeland. She took the crib, playpen and high chair because by this time I had a little brother named Mark. Mark was only three months old when we moved to Calgary. My dad was going to begin working in the oil patch, and my mom was going to be a stay at home mom. At that time my mom could speak only a bit of English.

When I was five, my dad enrolled me in minor hockey with the Trails West Minor Hockey Association in Calgary. I played one year with Trails West then we moved to an even bigger house that had a bigger yard and a cul-de-sac out front. My mom loved the house and even now that Mark and I are older and have moved out my parents still live in the same home. After the move, I started playing for the South Four Minor Hockey Association.

My dad was a great hockey dad. He took me to all my games and practices and cheered me on. He supported my drive to excel at the game and he even coached me one year. One day, I'd like to be a dad and take my children to their sporting events. But not right now. I'm too busy and love my life because I get to travel all over the place.

My brother and I would often have all our friends over for great street hockey games that would go all day. We would gather out front of our house, choose teams and set up our nets in the quiet cul-de-sac where little car traffic interrupted our game. We were always hitting the ball on our neighbour's lawn and my mother would get phone calls complaining. My parents were good about it though.

My brother, Mark, enjoyed playing hockey with us and is still such a good hockey player. He played for the Calgary Canucks Junior A team and then he also played for two years with the University of Wisconsin Badgers. After that he came back to Canada and played three years for the University of Toronto Varsity Blues. Recently, he graduated and signed a two-year contract to play hockey in Munich, Germany. I'm proud of my brother.

My brother and I have always had our hockey heroes. When I was growing up we lived a very comfortable life but my parents didn't have the extra money for us to attend Calgary Flames games so I watched them on television. I had a Calgary Flames Joe Mullen jersey that I just loved and I always wore it when I played road hockey. I can still remember the night I went to my very first NHL hockey game. The game was at the Saddledome and Calgary was hosting the St. Louis Blues. At that time, Wayne Thomas was the assistant coach for the Blues and he was a friend of my dad's. They had gone to college together in Wisconsin. Wayne got in touch with my dad before the game and gave him two tickets. I was so excited to go to an NHL hockey game! Then, at the end of the game, my dad surprised me and took me downstairs to meet Brett Hull and get his autograph. That night I became a big Brett Hull fan and I sort of switched teams as well and became a Blues fan. Brett is still someone I admire.

My brother and I would often have all our friends over for great street hockey games that would go all day.

It was always my dream to play in the NHL. But I also played hockey because it was fun and I loved it. I think it's important to play hockey for fun. If you're not having fun, you'll never excel.

I always tried my best and I guess I was lucky in my novice, atom and peewee hockey years because I played for a smaller minor hockey organization and I always made the first team.

My dad always told me, "Dany, just take it year by year." And I did.

I really loved playing baseball, too, so every summer when hockey was over, I played baseball. I was a catcher.

As a young teen, I didn't grow quite as quickly as some of my friends. I was what everyone called a 'late bloomer.' When I hit bantam, I knew that a lot of people didn't have faith in me—they didn't think that I had what it took to go anywhere in hockey. It's hard to play hockey at the bantam level when you're small, so I didn't make Bantam AAA in my first year, when I was 14 years old.

I don't like it when people criticize me. Few of us do, but when criticized, I tend to ignore the negative comments and the people who say them. What good would it do to listen to them? I just tell myself to show them I can succeed. My mom always said to my dad, "If anyone criticizes Dany, he just says I'm going to show them." And that is true. So I decided to try to show all those people who said I wasn't big enough and fast enough.

Despite my size, I made the Bantam AAA team and had a pretty good season at 15, though I was overlooked at the draft. They all said I was too small and too slow. One player from my team was drafted and went fifth overall. He and his family jumped up and down screaming with excitement.

I decided then that I would keep trying. I felt like I had something to prove and would show everyone who doubted me. I wasn't going to let something like not get drafted in bantam get me down. That's crazy. I had so many more years of hockey in me. And for me hockey was still really fun. I loved playing and wasn't going to quit.

Then things changed and I started to grow. That summer I grew six inches. It seemed that every time my dad or mom checked my height I had grown another inch. I also started to gain strength.

In the fall, I showed up to the Midget AAA hockey tryouts a totally different hockey player. For all you small players reading

This is my individual photo when I played for the South Four Minor Hockey
Association in Calgary.

A family photo. Me, my dad, Murray, my mom, Karin, and my brother, Mark.

this book, you have to give yourself time to grow. That next fall I was 6'1" and still growing. Suddenly, the coaches stood up and took notice.

I don't think they could believe it was actually me. The coaches said things to my dad like, "Is that really Dany Heatley? How come we overlooked him in the spring?"

All the skills that I had learned over the years just connected because I was stronger. My skating had improved and I was shooting the puck a lot harder. People came up to my dad and said, "He should have been drafted last spring." At that time Pat Matsuoka from the Red Deer Rebels talked to my dad and told him he was interested in me even though I hadn't been drafted.

I made the Midget AAA Calgary Buffaloes team. It was a good assembled team and as a group of guys we got along well. I loved playing on that team and because I was with such good hockey players, I had what everyone called, 'my breakout year.' Suddenly, everything started to click for me.

My Calgary Buffaloes team went on to win the provincials in Alberta, giving us a berth into the Canadian Midget AAA tournament called the Air Canada Cup. This is the tournament that decides the top Midget AAA team in Canada. Held in Sudbury that year, my team won the bronze medal—the best a Calgary team had done in years. That year I scored 90 points in 33 games. When the season ended, there were a lot of scouts talking to me and my dad. (My mom always let my dad handle the hockey stuff in my life, although I know my dad always consulted with her later, anyway.)

The Red Deer Rebels of the Western Hockey League invited me to their rookie training camp. The scouts told me that going to the WHL was a big step toward the pros and that this was my big break.

"Is that really Dany Heatley? How come we overlooked him in the spring?"

Sure, I was excited to be getting so much attention, but I wasn't sure if I wanted to play major junior hockey and leave home just yet. I also knew that if I played for Red Deer then I wouldn't be eligible for a college scholarship. Believe it or not, I liked school, especially math. I thought that since my father had played hockey on a scholarship that maybe I should take the same route.

This was such a big decision to make. Should I go play for the Red Deer Rebels and move away from home and billet with an unfamiliar family for my grade twelve year? Or should I stay at home, attend E.P. Scarlett High School, graduate with my friends, and pursue a scholarship to a university in the United States?

Big Decision, Big Payoff

U nsure of what I should do, I attended the Red Deer Rebels Major Junior rookie camp for two days as that was the limit without losing college eligibility. Before I stepped on the ice with Red Deer, I had talked to Don Phelps, coach of the Calgary Canucks, a Junior A team. Don seemed to really want me on his team but he also told me that he only wanted what was best for me.

"This is your decision," he said to me and my dad. We had met Don for pizza at Nick's restaurant in Calgary. "I am not going to try and convince you to play for me. This is something you have to decide as a family, as a household and..." Don paused and he looked me in the eye instead of my dad and said, "as an individual."

I think I might have nodded. I felt so young to be making such big decisions.

Fortunately, my dad patted me on the shoulder. "It will all work out," he said to me, "the way it's supposed to." My dad was trying to ease my mind.

On the second day of the Red Deer camp, I knew I was doing well. I'm not sure how I knew, but I just did. Sometimes that happens. I was scoring goals and skating as hard as I could.

After the two days at camp, I sat down with my mom and dad at the kitchen table, and we talked. My dad told me that the Red Deer coach wanted me. I didn't know what to do. If I went to Red Deer I'd have to leave home, stay with another family and switch high schools. I'd also have to do my homework on a bus most of the time. All WHL teams do a lot of bus travel.

Deep down, I guess I knew I didn't want to play Major Junior. Maybe I wasn't ready to leave home or my friends just yet. I wanted to graduate at my Calgary high school.

The biggest factor, however, was that I wanted to go to college and get an education. As I sat with my mom and dad I remembered all too well a family trip we had taken to Madison,

◀ *A move I tried at my first IIHF World Junior Championship in Sweden. (2000). Canada won the bronze medal that year.*

Wisconsin, even though it had been a few years back. I was twelve and playing for the Alberta Selects summer team. We had gone to a tournament in Minneapolis—St. Paul and when the tournament was over my dad suggested that we drive to Madison, which was only a few hours away. My dad still had lots of friends in Madison from his college days.

I sat in the back seat of the car with my brother, Mark. Even though we fought sometimes, we were excited to be on summer vacation and taking a family road trip. When we arrived in Madison the city was full of so much energy because it was Band Week. High school marching bands from all over the USA had come to Madison to compete against each other. We don't have the big marching bands in Canada like they do in the States. It's such a big deal down there. It was so awesome.

Neither of my parents knew it was Band Week. The city was jammed to capacity with visitors. We looked and looked for some kind of accommodation and, after a lengthy search, we finally found a motel room. We then went to the college to take in the festivities, and I remember the best part of the trip being when my dad let Mark and I sneak onto the big Camp Randall Stadium field where the University of Wisconsin football team played.

Remembering that trip and the excitement I had felt that day helped me make my decision. I knew what I wanted to do. I would play for the Calgary Canucks and not go to Red Deer. My parents agreed with me and encouraged me in my desire to get a scholarship. I know my dad was happy with my decision, as he too had gone to college. My dad always told me, "if all else fails, you can always get an education."

Additionally, there were other reasons that helped me make my decision to stay home, instead of heading to Red Deer. My family was so important to me and I guess to be honest with myself, I really didn't want to move away at that young age. I liked being at home with my mom and dad and Mark and they were pleased with my decision as none of them wanted to see me move out just yet. My mom talked to me about what it was like to be in an unfamiliar place with unfamiliar people and how she had been lonely when moving from Germany to Canada. I think she was afraid that if I moved away, I, too, would experience that loneliness.

While my dad taught me things about hockey, my mom taught Mark and me how to cook and, believe it or not, because of her teaching, I'm actually pretty skilled in the kitchen.

When it was just my dad, Mark, and I alone at home we made B.E.L.T. (bacon, egg, lettuce, tomato) sandwiches. But I think some of my favourite meals are my mom's Italian dishes like lasagna, and, of course, her German food, too.

So, home life helped me decide to take a spot on the Junior A Calgary Canucks and from the first day I showed up at practice, I knew it was the right decision.

I wasn't the most vocal guy on the team because I was younger, but I was keen. I was the first player on the ice and the last player off. I enjoyed every moment at the rink. Don was a great coach and I tried to listen to what he had to say so I could improve my game.

> *My family was so important to me and I guess to be honest with myself, I really didn't want to move away from them ...*

My Calgary Canucks team had a good season that year. My friend Moe Halat and I scored quite a number of the goals and my team ended up winning the Alberta league against St. Albert in a 4-0 sweep. I scored three back-to-back hat-tricks. Scoring goals is my passion! After the sweep, we boarded the bus to go to Vernon to play in the Western finals.

That was such a tough series. Every time I stepped on the ice I was shadowed by a Vernon player. They kept two guys on me at all times. Some guys get mad when that happens but I really tried hard to keep my cool. I just kept trying to get the puck and create some offence rather than take a stupid penalty. An exciting moment from the series was in the first game and we were down by a goal with just over a minute left to play and then we got a penalty. Don Phelps pulled the goalie anyway which was a really risky move. Then I tipped in a point shot, getting a short-handed goal to tie the game. During that game, I just kept shooting. That's the key to the game of hockey—keep shooting. My dad always said, "If you don't shoot, you can't get the puck in the net."

Unfortunately we lost in that playoff round against Vernon in five games and didn't make it to the RBC Cup. In total, the stats say that I scored 43 points in 18 playoff games.

During that year I managed to gain some recognition.

Often when we stopped and got off the bus, scouts were there to ask me questions. Sometimes this can be hard especially when I was trying to focus for the game ahead. I tried not to let any of the attention bother or rattle me or take me off my game.

I know the scouts were talking to Don about my skating, how I wasn't fast enough, and one day when I was chatting with Don he said to me, "The scouts are asking about your skating." Then he winked at me. "I always tell them that you skate from the opposing net to centre ice better than anyone I know.'"

Of course, what Don meant was that after I scored I could skate really well from the goal to centre for the faceoff. I laughed when he said that. I scored 70 goals in 60 games and my team had a 50-8-2 record. It was a great year!

I was so surprised when I won the Canadian Jr. Player of the Year trophy at the end of my Calgary Canucks season. I certainly wasn't expecting to get that award. It was a big thrill for me.

During that Canucks season, the college offers started to come in. At first, my dad thought it would be great if I attended an Ivy League school in the States. Ivy League schools are known for their great academics and I had pretty good marks in school.

Here I am with the President of the Alberta Junior Hockey League, Kim Marsh. He had just presented me with the Canadian Junior Player of the Year award.

The first school I visited was Ohio State and I liked it a lot. Immediately following the visit, I remember that I said, "That's where I want to go."

Then I visited Wisconsin. The memories of my family trip to Madison made me realize that I really wanted to go to the same college that my father went to. My dad didn't tell me to go there; in fact, he said he wasn't going to influence my decision but would support me in whatever decision I made. So I made the choice by myself. After visiting Wisconsin, I didn't visit another school, even though I was allowed to have five visits in total. I knew I didn't need to see any more schools.

After my season with the Calgary Canucks I got a phone call from Barry Trapp. Barry's nickname was Trapper. Trapper was the Hockey Canada Director of Scouting for the National Junior (under-20) Team that plays in the IIHF World Junior Championship which is held annually over Christmas and New Year's. I was excited when he called and invited me to try out for Canadian National Junior team. Most of the 40 players who were asked to the selection camp were the best players from Major Junior teams. I hadn't played Major Junior.

I felt right at home during the first practice and made it through the first round of cuts that happened at the end of the camp in August. The remaining players were invited to come to another camp in December and at that camp the coaches would decide which players would represent Canada and travel overseas for the tournament.

By that fall, at the age of 18, I was now ready to leave home. I packed my bags and my parents drove me down to Madison. I said good-bye to them knowing that I had made the right choice. I really did want to go to college because although I loved hockey, I knew that I wanted an education.

From the first day of orientation, I liked college. Campus life was so fun. Off the ice, I liked all my classes and I loved the atmosphere of being a student. On the ice, I fell right into being a player on the University of Wisconsin Badgers team. There were a lot of great guys on the team and the student body were huge supporters of their team.

I got lucky and was placed on a line with Steve Reinprecht. He was a senior when I was a freshman and he played centre on my line. Steve was considered one of the star players and a college veteran and now plays in the NHL for the Phoenix Coyotes. He's a great hockey player and I think we both felt an immediate on-ice chemistry from that first day of training camp.

Steve told me that after the training camp he had asked the coach if I could play on a line with him. Steve always told everyone that, "Dany loved to play hockey and he loved to score goals. He made my job easy." I was honoured that Steve spoke of me like that because he was such a good hockey player and someone who I admired and respected. I looked up to him as a leader.

Steve ended up winning the WCHA (Western Collegiate Hockey Association) scoring championship that year by racking up 66 points (26 goals and 40 assists).

As a rookie, I saw a lot of ice time, considerably more than most rookies. I think this is because I got to play on a line with Steve.

I flew back to Canada in December for the Christmas break when school was over. But instead of going home to Calgary, I attended the December National Junior Camp at the Beatrice Ice Gardens in Toronto.

To play for Team Canada in Sweden at Christmas would be the chance of a lifetime. Determined to show what I was made of, I skated with confidence. I wanted this opportunity to play for my country.

Off the ice, I liked all my classes and I loved the atmosphere of being a student.

I know that Trapper told everyone that, "Dany was picked for his offence." He also told everyone that the entire coaching staff was unsure of me because I had come out of Junior A and not Major Junior. Trapper told everyone, "We know he performed well, but we were concerned with his overall strength. But he had proved himself in the fall with the University of Wisconsin Badgers." Again, I was thankful that I had played with Steve.

Only two players playing college hockey were picked for the National Junior team, and I was one of them. Matt Pettinger, who played at the University of Denver, was added to the team roster late in December.

It was at the IIHF Junior Championship World that I met Jason Spezza. He's such a great guy and a great teammate. Jason was only 16-years-old at the 2000 IIHF World Junior

This is when I played college hockey for the University of Wisconsin Badgers.

Dominant Dany Heatley

Championship, and he became my linemate. We didn't score a ton of goals but we definitely had chemistry. I was kind of snake-bitten at the tournament which was frustrating. I hit so many posts and so did Jason, though one thing I learned was that I liked playing with him.

That year Canada won the bronze medal in a shoot-out against Russia. I took my bronze medal and returned to Wisconsin to finish off my year. And I had a great year. I managed to score 28 goals and 28 assists in 38 games.

Best of all, however, was that my team ended up winning the WCHA title.

That year, I was the first freshman forward to earn WCHA First Team honours since the 1970's and I was also an NCAA All-American. I was proud to earn those awards.

Then I was voted Rookie of the Year for the WCHA. I couldn't believe my good fortune and was pretty happy to get that trophy.

Then something new started to happen for me. NHL scouts started to look at me seriously. I had worked really hard to improve my skating because everyone always talked about what a poor skater I was. At that time I heard some weird rumours that some NHL scouts ranked me as the #1 draft pick!

Would I go #1 in the 2001 NHL draft?

To me that was a crazy thought.

At this point in my career, I wasn't even sure if I wanted to go to the NHL the following year. I loved playing college hockey. And I liked school, too. I liked being on campus and walking from class to class. I'd always dreamed of getting a college education.

My friend Steve Reinprecht understood me because he stayed in college for four years before making the jump to the NHL. College life was fun and Steve had enjoyed every minute of his four years. We talked about how we liked the atmosphere of campus life and the fun we had on our team.

Again, I knew some big decisions were coming my way.

THE BIG LEAGUES

I remember the morning of the 2000 NHL draft to this day. The June morning dawned, and it was a beautiful sunny day in Calgary, Alberta. The mountains to the west could be seen clear in the distance, standing tall and serene. My family arose and met downstairs for breakfast, knowing it was a special day and would have a significant impact on my life and future.

My parents were thrilled that the draft was being held in Calgary, our hometown. Now, they could be in attendance without having to spend money to fly somewhere.

I got dressed in the new suit that my parents had purchased for me just for that day. Then I combed my short hair. My mom had really wanted me to get my long hair cut for the draft, so I told her I would if she bought me a new suit. She didn't like my long college hair style.

We all got in the car and drove to the Saddledome. None of us talked in the car. Sitting in the packed stands at the arena, we all waited patiently. I remember being so uncomfortable in the seats and I kept fidgeting. First I'd sit forward then I'd sit back, and I just couldn't get comfortable. At that point I wondered where I would end up in the selection process. Some of my nervousness was the situation of waiting for my name to be called. But I was also nervous because even on that morning I still didn't know if playing in the NHL was what I wanted to do in the fall.

A buzz circulated among the spectators and hockey personnel who had shown up to watch the annual big event. I knew people were talking about me. "When do you think Heatley will go? Do you think Heatley will be first pick?" I was a Calgary boy and so with the draft being held in my hometown, I received a lot of attention and in some weird way, I become somewhat of a hometown hero, which made the pressure to make my decision to play in the NHL even greater. What would the media say if I decided to go to college?

◀ *My first NHL team was the Atlanta Thrashers.*

The first name called in the first round was goalie Rick DiPietro. Rick walked to the stage and put on his New York Islanders jersey.

The Atlanta Thrashers had the second pick in the first round. When my name was called, my parents grinned. Of course, I did too. I was honoured to be picked second overall. I approached the stage and proudly put on the Thrashers jersey. Then I posed for photos in the bright lights of the television cameras. I had never seen so many cameras in all my life.

This was an incredibly big day for me and for all young hockey players. Getting drafted is a lifelong dream for any player who has worked hard with the drive to play in the NHL. And I had been selected second in the first round of the NHL draft. People congratulated me afterwards and kept telling me that I had hit the big times.

That night when I went to sleep, I tossed and turned. I wanted to go the NHL, but I wanted to play college hockey, too. I couldn't stop thinking about my dream of getting an education.

It took me a few weeks to make my decision. And it wasn't easy. My parents avoided the discussion, which was good as admittedly I think I might have been a bit cranky to live with during those few days. While my family was incredibly proud of me, none of us talked too much in my house those days as they were purposely keeping quiet to allow me to make my decision. By this time I also had advisors, Stacey McAlpine and J.P. Barry, who were working for me. At that time, I couldn't have an agent if I was to stay in college. So my advisors were to negotiate my contract *if* I decided to go to the NHL. But if I decided to go to school then they couldn't work for me because college players weren't allowed to have agents. Stacey tried really hard not to influence my decision.

Finally, at breakfast a few days after the draft, I said to my parents, "I'm not going to Atlanta. I'm going back to Wisconsin for another year."

My parents looked at each other over their coffee, knowing that I had come to this huge decision on my own.

"We will support your decision," my father said.

Some in the hockey world couldn't figure me out. It was one thing to play Junior A instead of Major Junior but to turn down a NHL contract.... I know a lot of people thought I was being crazy. Not many hockey players turn down NHL contracts to go back to school.

I had my parents' total support and that was so important to me.

My mom told me, "You have made a very mature decision." She knew that I wasn't ready for the NHL. They supported me 100%.

And my dad told me, "That's a good decision. We're proud of you, Dany. You have your head on right."

That summer, before I headed back to school, I got another phone call from Hockey Canada. For the second year in a row, I had been picked to attend the National Junior Team selection camp that was happening in August. The tournament was at Christmas again, as it is every year, but that year it was in Moscow, Russia. I can't tell you how much I love playing for my country. I felt it was a huge honour to be asked to play on the Junior Team again. One day, I aspired to play for Team Canada in the Olympics. I went to the August camp and was reunited with some of the players, like Jason Spezza, from the team from the year before.

I can't tell you how much I love playing for my country.

In the fall, I returned to Madison, Wisconsin. Steve Reinprecht was no longer on our team, as he had finished his four years of eligibility and was now playing in the NHL for the Los Angeles Kings. I missed him a lot as did the team. I guess the opposing teams thought I was a threat offensively because game after game they were out to get me. Every game, I was physically pounded. There were times when I wondered if I'd made the right decision to come back to college hockey.

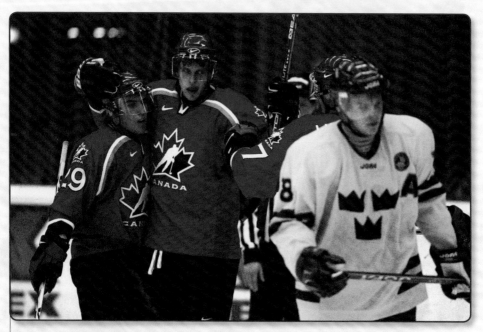

I made a lot of good friends when I played for Team Canada. 2001 IIHF World Junior Championship.

I love playing offensive hockey. 2001 IIHF World Juniors.

At that time I had to change the way I played. I remembered what Don Phelps had told me just a few short years before my college days when I'd asked what I needed to do to get better. He had told me to, "Improve your game when you don't have the puck."

Without Reinprecht there to feed me the puck, I had to work on many other aspects of my game. It was a tough year. I knew I had tons of obstacles to overcome.

When my team, the Badgers, started struggling, the media started rumours. They said I was going to quit school and go to Atlanta. Some reporters even said I might go home to Canada and play for the Red Deer Rebels.

I tried not to let any of that bother me. I had made a decision to go to school, and I was going to finish this year. In the spring, after classes were over, I would decide my future in hockey.

That Christmas I traveled to Moscow with the Canadian National Junior Team and we picked up another bronze medal. One day I wanted a gold medal.

I returned to school in January and every game I had two players checking me. Every time I stepped on the ice, I got hammered. But I didn't want to let my team down so I tried to push past the guys who were attacking me to score some goals. I still managed to have a decent scoring record. I scored 26 goals and 31 assists to make my total one point higher than the year before.

I finished my spring exams and I finally knew it was time to talk to my parents and Stacey about my future.

The time had come. I wanted Stacey to begin negotiations with the Atlanta Thrashers.

I was ready to play in the NHL.

I signed with Atlanta in April and packed my clothes and books, leaving my college dorm, knowing I wasn't returning to school. Right away that spring, I started to practice with Atlanta. I didn't dress and play, but I did spend the rest of the spring travelling with the team. On most of the road trips, I roomed with veteran Ray Ferraro.

Ray and I got along right away. I think he liked me because I wasn't scared of the older guys. I respected them too much to be afraid of them. I just wanted to learn from them.

I loved the NHL life right away and looked forward to the fall when I got to play with the team. I liked the travel, hotels and excitement that went with playing in the NHL.

I think I might have been Ray's messiest roommate. I used to drop my stuff wherever. But Ray never got mad at me. And I loved his kids. They were twelve and nine when I came to Atlanta and I always made time for them. They were great kids just like their dad. I think they liked me too because they always seemed excited to see me.

That summer I attended the Atlanta Thrashers rookie camp. It was during that camp that J.P. Vigier, a teammate of mine, accidentally high-sticked me. Blood spurted from my mouth, and my front tooth fell to the ice. The Atlanta trainer booked a dentist appointment for me and the dentist made a false tooth, though I have never liked playing with it in because it seemed to always fall out. I still don't like that tooth and often, after practices and games, I would forget to put it in when I left the dressing room. The media loved to take pictures of me without that tooth and I quickly became the hockey player with no front tooth.

The Atlanta Thrashers were a new NHL franchise when I signed with them. In fact, they had only been in the NHL for three seasons. They were looking for young players who could mature with the team and hopefully get them a berth into the playoff round in a few years time. They knew it would take time and they were willing to give us young players a few years to develop into good NHL players.

The prior year in Wisconsin, playing without Steve Reinprecht, I had become a better all-round player. I had worked hard to change my game. NHL players are always, always working on perfecting their game.

It wasn't long before I was on a line in Atlanta with another rookie player named Ilya Kovalchuk. Ilya was from

Russia. He was such a good hockey player and I loved playing with him.

Ilya and I had immediate chemistry on the ice. We became good friends, too, and rented condos in the same neighbourhood. The media painted a picture of us, calling us the "Gold Dust Twins." I think they named us that because they thought we were two gems that had been found but I don't know for sure. Sometimes the media are pretty creative with their descriptions. In December 2001, we were both named the NHL Rookie of the Month which was an honour. I was happy to share it with my teammate and my friend.

The Olympics in February 2002 were held in Salt Lake City, Utah, and I was disappointed to be overlooked as one of the players for Team Canada. Many sports personalities had speculated that I might be one of the players on the initial selection roster. Hockey Canada put together an incredible team for those games, so not being chosen was easier to accept. I didn't want to let this get to me and would use this disappointment to push me greater so that one day I would have my chance to play for Canada at the Olympics.

My linemate, Ilya Kovalchuk, popped the puck in the net six times. He was on fire that game.

Just prior to the Olympic Games at the NHL All-Star break, I was chosen to play in the YoungStars game. What fun that was. I managed to get a goal and two assists. My linemate, Ilya Kovalchuk, popped the puck in the net six times. He was on fire that game.

Ilya and I became a dynamic duo and every game we stepped on the ice we played as hard as we could. We kept performing and found ourselves in a race for the Calder Trophy, which is the trophy for the best rookie in the NHL. It was rare in NHL history that two rookies, playing on the same line, for the same team, were viable contenders for the Calder Trophy. Usually rookies were positioned with veterans to help them

This was at the 2002 IIHF Men's World Championship. We lost in the quarter-finals that year.

along, so I was glad that my Atlanta coach, Curt Fraser, put us — two rookies — together on a line.

I finished that first season in the NHL with 67 points. I had 41 assists and 26 goals. Those stats put me at the top of the heap for rookie players. I had the most points, assists, and shots for all first-year players and I was tied for the lead in power-play goals. I don't know how I did that but I did. I just played as hard as I could and went to the net like my coach told me to do. I was disappointed when the Atlanta Thrashers didn't make the playoffs. It meant an early summer for me.

Spring may have sprung in Atlanta, but back home in Canada it was still cold, too cold for my hockey season to be over. When I got the phone call from Lanny McDonald, the GM of the Canadian Men's World Championship team and a former Calgary Flames player, I was pumped. Lanny wanted me to play for Team Canada at the IIHF Men's World Championships in Karlstad, Sweden. I immediately packed my equipment and some clothes and jumped on a plane.

The odds weren't in Canada's favour at this tournament. Over 60 players declined an invitation to play for their country for a number of reasons. Some had won gold for Canada in the 2002 Olympics and were injured, tired, or they just said no. I felt that if Team Canada called it was an honour and a privilege. There was no way I was going to turn down the offer to wear the red and white jersey and represent my country on the world stage.

The Canadian team lost out to Slovakia, 3-2, in a tight quarter-final game. It was a devastating loss. Back home in Canada the media said that we lost because of a lack of effort from many players. Playing an entire season, plus appearing at an Olympic tournament all in one year is a grueling and exhausting schedule, so I don't agree with those accusations. The mood in the dressing room the night that we lost was somber. So far for Team Canada, I had two bronze medals from my World Junior experiences. One day, I wanted a gold medal from a world competition. I knew I would just have to keep trying and say yes every time I was invited to play.

I felt that if Team Canada called it was an honour and a privilege

I didn't dwell on the loss for very long because at the NHL awards banquet in June of 2002 I won the Calder Trophy.

I think I came out on top because Ilya injured his shoulder and missed a few games. I would have been happier if Ilya and I had shared the honours but there could only be one winner.

TROPHIES AND MEDALS

After spending some time at home relaxing and hanging out with friends and family, I returned to Atlanta in the fall. The 2002/2003 season started off a bit slow and I found myself in the middle of a scoring drought. I'm not sure what was happening or why I couldn't score. I kept hammering and hammering, trying to score, but nothing seemed to work. I tried to play strong defensively but this made me struggle with my offence. I kept telling myself not to get frustrated and to just keep trying. I didn't want to be known as a person who would give up easily.

Finally, in January, I hit my stride again and scored 13 goals in one month. I scored my first career hat trick on January 12th in a game against Philadelphia. The hat trick helped break our 12-game losing streak. Then, I celebrated my 22nd birthday on January 21st with two power-play goals in a game against the St. Louis Blues. After meeting Brett Hull when I was young, the Blues had become my favourite team, so it was great to beat them on my birthday. We won that game, 8-4.

I was back on the stats sheet, playing offensive hockey, which seemed to be my specialty.

My game had improved, and, as a result, I was asked to represent Atlanta for the Eastern Conference Team at the annual NHL All-Star game. And when I pulled that jersey over my head in Sunrise, Florida, I did so with a sense of pride, though was totally unaware of what lay ahead for me. I loved playing hockey and felt privileged to be part of a team with such impressive veteran NHL players. I thought that maybe, since there were such good passers on my team, I might get some shots on net. I was playing with some of the most skilled players in the NHL.

Maybe, just maybe I would get a goal. To shoot and see the red light just once in an All-Star game was a dream. One goal, that's all I wanted. Marty Turco had been one of the goalies selected to play for the Western Team and he was familiar

◀ *We won the gold medal at the 2003 IIHF World Championship in Finland. It was my first Team Canada gold medal.*

to me. I had played with Marty the spring before at the IIHF Men's World Championships. I hoped I could beat him just once. The other goalies for the Western team were Patrick Roy and Jocelyn Thibault. Roy was considered the best goalie in the league and was an amazing goalie.

I blasted on the ice and skated around in warm-up. I felt relaxed. I was shocked when I scored the first goal of the game at the 5:39 mark of the first period, beating Patrick between the pads. I really thought that I had just had a lucky shot.

Soon after my goal, the West scored and this put my team down by a goal. Then at 10:26 of the first period, I managed to somehow bat a puck out of the air, beating Patrick again. I attributed my second goal to another lucky break and considered myself fortunate to have not one but two goals.

In the second period, we were up against Chicago's goalie, Jocelyn Thibault. I was having one of those games where everything just seemed to click. My luck kept coming. In that period I scored another two goals to make my total four!

When my team filed into the dressing room between the second and third period there was a buzz about me breaking the scoring record which stood at four goals. At that point in the game I was tied with Vincent Damphouse, Mike Gartner, Wayne Gretzky and Mario Lemieux – all of whom had scored four goals in an All-Star contest. I couldn't believe that I was even on the same page as these amazing hockey players.

Wayne Gretzky visited our dressing room during that second intermission and said he was cheering for me – hoping that I would break the current record. When I stepped on the ice for the third period, Marty Turco was in net for the West. Every player on my line passed the puck to me, trying to help me break the record.

But Turco stayed so solid in net and I didn't score in the third period.

I didn't break the scoring record, but I did break the record for youngest player to score four goals. When Wayne Gretzky scored his four goals he had been 22 and 13 days old. When I broke the record I was 22 and 12 days old. I beat Wayne by one day to be the youngest ever to score four goals in an NHL All-Star game. How could I have beat Wayne Gretzky? To me that is such a crazy record to break.

At the end of the game, the score was tied and we headed into an exciting shootout. I scored the only goal for the East team, though since the goal occurred in a shootout, it wasn't included with the previous four to break the record.

After the game, it was announced that I had won the tournament All-Star game MVP trophy! I was so happy to win that I forgot to put my false tooth in for my media interviews. My toothless smile was displayed on every sports page and sports networks that night and the next day.

Throughout the game, Philadelphia Flyers player, Jeremy Roenick, had been wearing a microphone while playing, so he could commentate for ABC. He was on the same team as me. He kept talking about how well I was playing. Jeremy was quoted as saying, "He is only going to do good things for our league. He's a better person than he is hockey player." That was a very big compliment and I really appreciated what he said, especially the stuff about me being a good person. My parents always taught me that being a good person came before being a good hockey player.

> "He is only going to do good things for our league. He's a better person than he is hockey player."
>
> [Jeremy Roenick]

After that All-Star game, I suddenly became a player that some fans came to watch. When the Atlanta Thrashers arrived in an opposing city for a game, fans lined up to get my autograph. This was a strange because I was just a normal guy who liked to play hockey.

That spring, the Thrashers, once again, failed to make the playoffs. Next year, next year, I kept telling myself. I really liked playing for Atlanta and wanted to be on the team next year when they made the playoffs. Now, I had friends on the team and I liked the management and coaching staff at Atlanta. I managed to finish my second season as the top Atlanta scorer with 89 points: 41 goals and 48 assists.

Although my NHL season was over, it wasn't quite time for me to hang up my skates for the year as I would be again representing Canada at the IIHF Men's World Championships. This time I boarded a plane with my brother, Mark, to make the long flight to Helsinki, Finland.

That World Championship team that Hockey Canada assembled for the 2003 Worlds clicked. Our team wasn't stacked with big name players, like the 2002 Olympic Team that won the gold medal, but we were a working team. We had great chemistry and all bonded.

I loved being part of that team. The guys were fun and I was thrilled to play with my University of Wisconsin teammate, Steve Reinprecht again. The games were fast and furious, though I started off the tournament a bit slower than I would have liked.

Canada racked up three early wins showing the strength of our team. We beat Belarus 3-0, Latvia 6-1, and Sweden, 3-1. Then we played to a 2-2 tie with Denmark. We all went back to the dressing room thinking about that tie. There was no way we should have come away with a tie because we were clearly a better team and we should have easily won. We all realized that to win a gold medal we needed to dig a little deeper. I had been picking up the odd point here and there and had definitely been a contributor to the team, but I certainly wasn't the force that I wanted to be. My strength is my offence, so if I'm not scoring, I'm not doing my job.

For the next two Canadian victories, I went into a mini-scoring slump. I was frustrated with my own play but happy with the team's play. We won both games so I didn't take it too hard but I did want to start scoring to help my team. I knew the

I had so much fun at the NHL All-Star Game in Florida in 2003. I won the MVP trophy that year.

Stacey and I in the Okanagan. (Summer 2008.)

coach of the team, Andy Murray, picked me for my goal scoring. After that tie we beat the Swiss, 2-0, and the Russians, 5-2, and I didn't pick up one point in those two games.

But we had advanced to the quarter-finals and would meet Germany. The quarter-finals is the toughest game in the Championships because even if you have won every game, losing that game means you are done and your team goes home the next day. No way did any of us want to go home. We were having way too much fun and we came to win!

We took an early lead against the German team and being over confident we started playing sloppy and allowed them to tie the game. I remember looking up at the scoreboard and seeing that 2-2 score. How could we have lost a two-goal lead? There was no way we wanted to lose this game and go home. We had to win.

Then the game just became one of those games where the puck went up and down the ice. The Germans were on a high from tying the game up and were trying to beat us along the boards. For them to beat the Canadians and move on the semi-finals would be huge for the German hockey program.

My game clicked and I scored a hat trick leading our team to an 8-4 victory!

We fought back. With just seconds left in the game, we scored! I tell you that game made us think. Yes, we had a berth to the semi-finals, but we had barely won.

We were going to have to play a lot better in our semi-final game against the Czech Republic if we were to succeed.

We knew we had almost lost out in the quarter-final, so we arrived at that semi-final with determination. I had never played in the gold medal game at any World Championship and I wanted to win. I stepped on the ice full of confidence.

We played well. My game clicked and I scored a hat trick leading our team to an 8-4 victory! The win meant we would meet Sweden in the gold-medal game.

The winning team at the Men's IIHF World Championship in 2003.
Anson Carter scored in overtime.

Our team knew we had what it took to win the gold medal. We talked in the dressing room and there was a really good feeling among the guys.

On the day of the game, I could feel the butterflies in my stomach. I'd played big games before, but this was probably the biggest. I was playing for a gold medal – representing my country – at the IIHF Men's World Championship.

Sweden scored first. They were really pressuring our defence and our puck carriers. Then they scored again late in the period to take a 2-0 lead. That was tough. We talked on the bench. We had to get a goal before the period was over to gain some momentum. With just 43 seconds left in the first period, Shawn Horcoff scored for us to make the score 2-1.

That was a huge boost and we went to the dressing with momentum, confident that we could come back after the break and turn the game around. But there were no goals in the second period.

In the third period, still down 2-1, Horcoff made a beautiful pass to Shane Doan who popped it past the Swedish goalie. We were pumped. Now the game was tied! Canada was back in the game.

When the buzzer went to end the third period, the score was still tied. We were going to overtime. The rules stated that we would have a four-on-four 20-minute overtime period and if the score was still tied then we would go to a shootout. Every player on my team only played 20-30 second shifts to save their legs. The changes were continuous. Every time I hopped the boards to get on the ice, I was ready to give it my all. I liked the excitement and challenge. The Swedes were strong and pressured us, but our coaches had a great game plan.

When Anson Carter put the puck past the Swedish goalie at the 13:49 mark, in a wrap-around move, our team went crazy and were ready to jump the bench, but couldn't just yet, because the call went upstairs for video replay.

I waited very impatiently. We all kept waiting and waiting for the referee to make the sign that the goal counted. We stared up at the board, hoping to see the goal appear on the scoreboard, and then finally, the referee had the results.

I was playing for a gold medal – representing my country – at the IIHF Men's World Championship.

He put his hand down to tell us – and the world - that the goal was in! Canada had won gold!

I jumped off that bench so fast and threw my gloves in the air. Then I skated toward our goalie, Roberto Luongo, and the entire Canadian team surrounded him in celebration.

When they put the gold medal around my neck, I know I grinned from ear to ear. In moments like that it's hard to remember what you do because the adrenaline is just so strong and you feel so amazing.

I loved that feeling of winning on the world stage.

TWISTS AND TURNS

CHAPTER FIVE

The long overseas flight back to Calgary gave me time to sleep and reflect about my year. I'd worked hard. It had been a good year. But next year would be better. Atlanta was still a young team, but on the verge of cracking the regular season to get enough points to earn a berth in the playoffs.

Landing in Calgary, I smiled when I saw my mother and father waiting for me at the airport. They were still my biggest fans and I loved them for that. They were always so supportive and when I was young, and playing minor hockey, they were always at my games.

The long summer months were before me. I loved summer and looked forward to some golf, relaxing in the sun, and spending a lot of time in the gym. To stay in shape and remain competitive as a top player in the NHL takes work and dedication. There was no way I was going to rest on all the good things that had happened to me during the year. Sure I had won the MVP at the All-Star game, and sure I had won a gold medal with Team Canada, but that didn't mean I could settle for dogging it all summer. No athlete could. Things can change so quickly for any hockey player. I had to be in top shape when I showed up at training camp in the fall.

When I arrived at the Atlanta training camp I almost felt as if I'd returned home. When I walked in the dressing room it was as if I never left. There was a true sense of belonging. I was no longer the rookie trying to make the grade. Now I was part of this team. I had good friends who were teammates.

I laced up my skates and stepped on the ice ready for a new season.

This good feeling, unfortunately, didn't last long. I found out that life isn't always fair and that terrible things can happen to good people. I had lived my life till that point always trying to follow the right path. All my life, I'd been a good guy: coaches and teammates usually liked me, teachers liked me, and I never

◄ *Someone scored! For the second year in a row, we won gold at the IIHF Men's World Championship. This time the tournament was in Prague. (2004)*

rebelled against my parents. I worked hard and respected those around me, but none of that mattered. I was to be part of an horrific event that would change my life and end the life of someone incredibly important to me – my friend and teammate Dan Snyder.

One night after training camp, I was driving my car when I lost control and hit a brick pillar. I broke my jaw, and tore some of the ligaments in my knee. But that was that nothing because my good friend and Atlanta teammate, Dan Snyder, who was with me at the time, suffered severe injuries. At the time, I didn't care about my injuries because I was so worried about Dan. Six days after the accident, just when we thought Dan was doing better, he passed away. He was just 25-years-old. He was a talented hockey player and was loved and admired by many people. I was deeply saddened.

The family values that my mom and dad had given me so early in my life carried me through this horrible time. The media blew the story up and concocted many different versions of what happened, and most of the stories were inaccurate. I tried not to read what they said. I felt fortunate that I had my mom and dad and my brother Mark to support me. They were beside me at all times. I also had tremendous support from Stacey, my agent. Stacey was able to help me and my parents through the legalities and personal challenges that resulted from the accident.

The doctors told me that I wouldn't play hockey for the rest of the season. This was not what I wanted to hear. To feel alive, I needed to play hockey. The rehabilitation process was gruelling, but I worked as hard as I could. I did everything the doctors said, and more. Although I spent weeks in the hospital and missed the first 51 games of the season, I was given the green light to play again in January. The doctors were impressed with my determination and work ethic and were shocked that I had healed as fast as I had. My parents weren't shocked though.

Me, Bouwmeester and Niedermayer hugging after scoring.
(2004 IIHF Men's World Championship in Prague.)

They told me they knew I would be determined to get back on the ice.

It felt good to play hockey again and I managed to score 12 goals and 13 assists for a total of 25 points in 31 games.

That spring when Atlanta didn't make the playoffs again, I went home to Calgary. I was glad to land in Calgary. When I got the call to go overseas with Team Canada, my heart picked up speed again and I realized that no matter what, I still wanted to play hockey. This year the IIHF Men's World Championships were held in Prague, in the Czech Republic.

Hockey Canada is really good about letting players bring members of their family along to the World Championships. I really wanted my family to come to Prague. I needed them with me.

I asked my mom and dad if they wanted to come with me. Prague was a beautiful city. I knew that they had just as tough a year as me. They had worried about me a lot. They agreed to come, thinking it might be a change of scenery and a nice holiday. Plus, my mom knew that while she was in Europe, she could go home to Germany for a visit. It would be good for her to see her family.

I also wanted Stacey to come to Prague. Stacey had become much more than just my agent. While he was there for me in my professional career negotiations, he had become a very true friend, someone I could trust without compromise. Stacey often came with me on trips, but he knew this trip was really important to me. I wanted him there with my family. He said yes without hesitation.

In our first game of the tournament, we tied Austria, 2-2. Austria is known more for their cross-country skiers than hockey players so that was a bit of a letdown for us. In fact, a tie for the Canadian team was terrible. We knew we had to do a lot better if we were going to win another gold medal.

In the dressing room we talked and got ourselves motivated which seemed to help. We won our next three games, beating

France, 3-0, Switzerland, 3-1, and Latvia, 2-0. Walking to the dressing room after the Swiss game, I knew I had to play better if we were to win the gold medal. I had been picking up the occasional point but nothing significant. We hadn't beaten any of those teams by very many goals. I had brought my parents to Prague and I wanted to give them something to smile about.

I stepped on the ice for the next game with determination. The Canadians were playing Germany. My mom sat in the stands and cheered for me, rather than for her home-country team. I was more important to her but then she had always put me and my brother first.

I had a great game and as a team we hit our stride. We embarrassed Germany, 6-1. It gave me great comfort to see my parents in the stands and to meet them after the games. During the day my mom and dad toured around Prague, enjoying the sites of such a fantastic city.

Our last qualifying game was against the Czech Republic. The hometown arena was packed. Over in Czech, they love their hockey. And the Czech hockey fans wanted to see their national team play well against the dominating Canadians. Team Canada is a big draw and whenever and wherever we play, fans come out to watch the team from the country that gave birth to the game of hockey. Everyone in Europe always wanted to see the Canadians play. The noise level in the arena was deafening. The Czech fans had cheerleaders and the fans whistled and screamed and jumped up and down in the stands.

I don't know what happened to us that night but we came out totally flat and we ended up losing, 6-2. The Czech fans went wild. At the end of the game, I hung my head because I just couldn't believe we had lost by four goals. Of course, it

> *We knew we had to do a lot better if we were going to win another gold medal.*

My dad always told me to get the puck and shoot.
(2004 IIHF Men's World Championship.)

didn't mean our team was out of contention, but it did mean we had to play a lot harder.

At the end of the qualification games, we met Finland in the quarter-final.

That game against Finland was tough. We rallied against them in what the fans would call a nail-biter. The score was tied 4-4 at the end of regulation time. We experienced overtime the year before at the IIHF World Championships, so we knew just how intense this extra period would be.

Every shift we all skated hard. It was one of those overtimes where the puck went up and down the ice. Then suddenly, I picked up a loose puck in the neutral zone, skated to the blue line and rifled it as hard as I could. When I saw it go in to the top corner and the red light go on, I jumped in the air. Everyone congratulated me! Man, it felt good to score like that and win. Even Wayne Gretzky took notice. To me that was huge because I knew he was going to be the General Manager for the Canadian World Cup team in the fall of 2004 and I was determined to make that team.

I don't know what happened to us that night but we came out totally flat and we ended up losing 6-2.

Our semi-final game was to be against Slovakia. Again it was another close, close game. But we ended up winning with a score of 2-1. This time when we filed to the dressing room after the game, we were totally pumped to play in the gold-medal game.

I knew that winning back-to-back gold medals was extremely difficult. In fact, Canada hadn't won back-to-back World Championships since 1958/59. My team was going to have to play Sweden again, just like the year before. We all knew it would be a tough game.

Sweden took the jump in the game and scored right off the bat. I think they scored within the first few minutes. Then they scored again. It was midway through the first period, and we were already down, 2-0. The fans in the building were going crazy, yelling and screaming.

When my teammate Ryan Smyth scored, we were back in the game. Smytty is a great guy and a player you can always depend on to get the job done. When Sweden scored another goal, it silenced our bench. I sucked in a deep breath knowing that my job was to play offensive hockey. I had been having a great tournament. I'd scored seven goals already, but I hadn't scored yet in that gold-medal game.

I stepped on the ice and set up at the faceoff circle. At the 14:44 mark in the second period, I got the puck on the end of my stick and let it rip. Okay, so now we only needed one to tie it up. Just one goal.

Then luck intervened for us and a Swedish player put the puck in his own net to make it a tie game. Sometimes things like that happen in intense hockey games and you learn how to say thanks. It was a true break for us. And sometimes this kind of incident can shift the momentum of the game.

This set us on fire and in the third period we scored two more goals. When the buzzer went in the third period, I looked at the score. We had won by one goal.

We had won the gold medal!

I loved lining up at the blue line and seeing our flag displayed and hearing the Canadian national anthem. All I could do was smile, along with all my teammates. It was such a great feeling. I'd had a good tournament and I was pleased with how I had played. I'd scored eight goals and 11 assists.

After they gave out the team medals, the announcer called me up to the front.

I was shocked to find out that I had won the MVP for the entire tournament!

When I looked to the stands to find my parents and Stacey, I found them proudly standing and cheering with huge smiles on their faces.

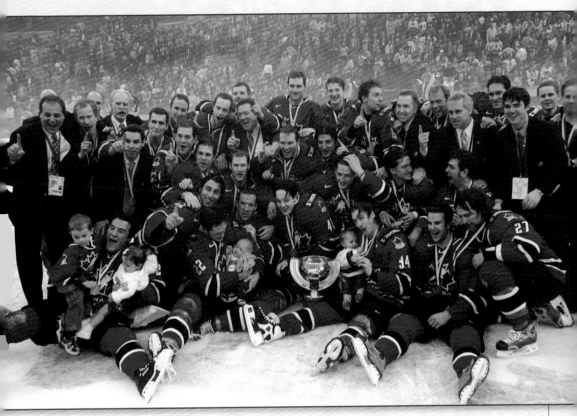

Team photo after winning the gold medal. (2004 IIHF Men's World Championship)

President of the IIHF, René Fasel, is giving me the MVP trophy at the 2004 Men's World Championship in Prague.

It had been a tough year for all of us. Finally, something good had happened.

During the summer, while trying to relax, I constantly listened to the sports news. There were major NHL disputes happening and there was talk that the NHL would have a lockout in the fall. If that happened there would be no NHL.

What would I do for the year with no hockey?

Then I was asked to tryout for Hockey Canada's World Cup Team. The tournament was to take place in Toronto, in September. This was a huge honour for me. I would be playing on the same team with the best players in the world. Wayne Gretzky was the General Manager along with Kevin Lowe and Steve Tambellini, and Pat Quinn was the coach along with Ken Hitchcock, Jacques Martin and Wayne Fleming. To play for all these great hockey men would be incredible. This team was like an Olympic team. I knew I was pretty young to be playing on such an important team with such a great management staff and such amazing veterans players.

I was shocked to find out that I had won the MVP for the entire tournament!

The tournament was everything I dreamed of. Canada had a flawless record at that 2004 World Cup. We won every game we played, winning the final game against Finland 3-2 in front of a sold out crowd at the Air Canada Centre. I ended up with two assists by the end of the tournament, which isn't great for me, but it didn't matter because the win was such a big high for everyone on the team.

During the tournament, in the dressing room before and after games and practices, we all talked about what we were going to do should there be an NHL lockout. The disputes had not been solved and the lockout definitely was a reality. I listened to everyone talk. Some of the married guys wanted to spend more time with their families and would work on getting ice time at home arenas. Some of the other players decided to train in the gym all year. I wasn't married and didn't have any children and I thought I might get a bit bored just training all the time. I felt I had to play games to keep up my skills. I had to play hockey. I knew what I wanted to do.

I was going to go to Europe and play in one of the European leagues just like my dad had done.

Right after World Cup, I decided that I would go to Switzerland to play hockey. Of course, my dad thought this was a great idea. He had loved playing in Europe. Europe would give me something different. They played a different style of hockey over there, and they played on the big ice surface. Maybe I would learn some new things.

I signed with a team in Bern, Switzerland. Bern was a small city located in the Swiss Alps. I liked the cobblestone lanes and the old buildings. After all the twists and turns I had been through in just one year, I found that I enjoyed the slower pace of Bern. It seems kind of strange because I like to be busy all the time, but Bern was different and I liked it. From September to November, I played in the European league. I traveled through Switzerland to many different cities and towns. Most of the European players were friendly and they didn't seem put out that a Canadian was on their team. I wasn't the only NHL player who decided to spend the season in Europe and we all felt welcomed by our new teams. I got along well with my linemate, Daniel Briere. We became good friends. That's one of the things I love about hockey—the good friends that you make.

All was going well until one game when I was skating down the right side of the rink with Daniel driving to the net. I wound up for a slapshot and fired the puck so hard that I totally spun around. Daniel picked up the rebound and rifled the puck as hard as he could. Because I was still spinning around I didn't have time to move and the puck hit me square in the eye.

Rushed to the hospital, I saw a doctor right away. They ran a lot of tests and I found out that I had an orbital bone fracture.

They said it would be best if I went home and got treatment by my own Canadian doctor. For days, I had to remain in Switzerland until my eye was healed enough so I could fly home. Once I was given the okay to travel, I boarded a plane. I had played 16 only games in Bern but I had scored 14 goals and ten assists. It really made me upset that I was going home with an eye injury and that it looked like my season was coming to an abrupt end.

I arrived in Canada and saw an eye surgeon. He told me I wouldn't play for the rest of the year.

The rest of the year!?

I remembered when I broke my jaw. So I knew what to do. I had to rehab as much as I could. The doctors were again amazed when my eye took only three months to heal. I believe if you want to get your body to heal you have to do everything the doctors say and never slack off from the exercises they give you.

> *Because I was still spinning around I didn't have time to move and the puck hit me square in the eye.*

In January, I decided to return to Europe but instead of going back to Bern, I signed with Ak Bars Kazan in Russia. This was a team that was already loaded with quite a few great NHL players.

One of the players was Ilya Kovalchuk, my good friend from my first days in Atlanta. I looked forward to playing with him again.

I flew over to Russia with Stacey and was delighted upon seeing my accommodations. We all stayed in a very nice, fancy hotel. There wasn't much else to do in Russia but play hockey. Kazan was a small city in the middle of nowhere. Outside the hotel, the air was cold, the land flat and barren. But that didn't bother me too much because the hockey was great. I enjoyed playing with such good NHL players. And my eye had fully healed.

I lived and played in Russia from February to April. When the season ended and I was about ready to fly home from Russia,

I got the call from Team Canada. This year the IIHF Men's World Championship was in Austria. Of course, I immediately said yes. I definitely wanted my season to continue.

Could Canada possibly win three World Championships in a row? That would be a great record. I would love to be part of such a dynasty.

Our team looked good. There was definitely the possibility of capturing gold again. If that was so, we would make history.

The tournament started off well for my Canadian team. We won our first three games and I have to admit that I got excited thinking that we might be headed to another gold-medal victory. In the preliminary round we established a good record with three wins, one loss and a tie. Then we won our quarter-final game against Slovakia, 2-1. In the semi-final game, we registered a huge win by beating the Russians 4-3 to advance to the gold medal game. The Russians had been one of the favoured teams.

For the third year in a row, I sat in a dressing room, ready to play for a gold medal for Canada. I couldn't believe it. I wanted to beat the Czech Republic badly. When the Canadians stepped on the ice in Vienna, Austria the fans screamed. But when the Czech team flew on the ice the fans went absolutely crazy! We were definitely not the favoured team. Busloads of people from the Czech Republic had arrived to watch the game.

We started off slow and Czech took advantage of this and we never found the net in that gold-medal game. The score was 3-0 for Czech Republic when the buzzer sounded at the end of the third period. I lined up at centre ice to accept my silver medal. That's when I got my first taste of a silver medal. It's a hard one to take because you get a medal after you have just lost a game.

The final twist in that year came in the summer.

My three-year contract had expired with Atlanta and I became a Group 2 restricted free agent. Atlanta made me an offer

Canada won the World Cup in 2004 in Toronto with an undefeated record. No wonder I'm smiling.

but it was for one-year only. I didn't really understand why they wanted to sign me for only one year. Somehow it didn't feel right. I turned to the people who could help me the most: my parents. Although Stacey McAlpine and J.P. Barry were my agents and it was their job to do my negotiations, it was I who had to decide what I should do. And at that time I really wanted my parents' input. Stacey and J.P. were great and only offered advice if I asked for it because ultimately they knew it wasn't their decision.

I sat down with my parents and discussed my decision based on hockey, business and my personal life. My parents thought it might be good for me to have a change of scenery and not live in Atlanta anymore. And I agreed with them.

On August 23, 2005, I was traded to the Ottawa Senators for Marian Hossa and Greg De Vries. I left Atlanta and headed north to Canada's capital city.

At my press conference in Ottawa, Chris Phillips, one of the Senators' top defencemen and an assistant captain for the team, was there for support. Chris took the time to show me around the dressing room and the Senators' offices. We quickly became good friends.

In September, I showed up at the Senators' training camp ready and able to play good hockey!

A new chapter in my life was beginning.

◄ *Holding the 2004 World Cup trophy over my head after we won the gold medal.*

OTTAWA AND THE OLYMPICS

From my first practice with the Senators, I knew the move to Ottawa had been a good one. I adjusted immediately to my new teammates and I liked Ottawa.

I was happy to be friends with Chris Phillips and he made me feel quite welcome. He kept telling me that the team was glad I was in Ottawa because everyone knew I liked to score goals.

Chris and I were assigned to be roommates.

The first game I played for the Senators was against the Toronto Maple Leafs on October 5th, 2005. The coach put me on a line with Jason Spezza and Brandon Bochenski. I was thrilled to be re-united with Jason, my friend from Canada's National Junior Team. Even though we played pretty well together, the Senators were still trailing in the last five minutes of the game. Then my coach put Daniel Alfredsson on instead of Brandon Bochenski.

The sparks flew! Immediate chemistry! It was great.

We worked amazingly well together and we put the pressure on the Leafs. When Alfredsson scored the tying goal, Jason and I rushed over to give him a group hug. Our line became known as the "CASH" line. The 'C' was for Captain, 'A' for Alfredsson, the 'S' was for Spezza, and the 'H' was for Heatley. That first game ended in a tie. After the overtime period, the game went to a shoot-out. This was the first year for the shootout in NHL hockey. And this was the first game to have a shootout situation.

That night, Alfredsson and I became the first NHL players to score in the shootout. Going against Leafs' goalie, Ed Belfour, I took the puck down and ripped off a low wrist shot that landed in the back of the net. After the game, the Hockey Hall of Fame wanted both our sticks. The sticks now reside in that hallowed hockey shrine in Toronto as the first sticks to score in an NHL shootout.

The year was definitely starting off in the right direction for me.

◀ *This was taken at the 2006 Olympic Games in Torino.*

I felt good and things started clicking. I quickly racked up points. I got points in the first 22 games of the season. To me that was amazing. I know so much of that success was because of the guys on my line. Hockey is a team sport. But the NHL loves to make records and fans love to read all about records. The only other player to score in more games than me when starting with a new team was Wayne Gretzky. I felt pretty darn honoured to be close to sharing a record like that with The Great One. Wayne scored in his first 23 games when he started with Los Angeles. I was just one behind him with my 22-games streak.

I felt a real passion for the game, and playing with the Senators was such fun. Chris and I had a blast on the road, sharing a room.

One game I really remember was on October 29, 2005. I scored four goals in a row to lead the Senators to an 8-0 win over the Toronto Maple Leafs!

That same year, Team Canada was picking its Olympic roster. I may have been too young and not experienced to play in Salt Lake City in 2002, but the Team Canada coaches now looked at me to be one of their stronger players for the 2006 Olympics. I had two gold medals from the World Championships but didn't have an Olympic gold medal yet. What would it be like to win an Olympic medal?

In February, I boarded the chartered flight that was leaving from Toronto and flying non-stop to Turino, Italy. All my teammates and the coaching and management staff of Team Canada were also on the plane. The team was stacked with many good players, including Jarome Iginla, Joe Sakic and Chris Pronger.

On paper our team looked like strong contenders for the gold medal. We also had the same proven coaching staff from the 2002 Olympic Gold medal team and from the World Cup. All in all we looked like a winning team.

On the ice, however, we never seemed to click. It was just one of those teams that didn't gel. To this day I can't tell

you what was wrong with that team, but something wasn't quite right.

I liked the Team Canada black jerseys. (2006 Olympics in Torino, Italy.)

When we were beaten in the quarter-finals by the Russians, I was extremely disappointed. My Olympic gold medal dream was over for another four years. I really hope that I get a shot at the Olympics again in 2010 in Vancouver.

I flew home from the Olympics tired and saddened by the loss, but that didn't stop me from getting right back into the Senators' stream. We all wanted to make our NHL year worth something. I managed to finish that season with 50 goals and 103 points. I was happy to get 50 goals. I ended up fourth in the NHL in scoring. I also set a Senators record for goals and became the first Senator to ever score 50 goals. But more than

that, the Senators ended with the best record in the Eastern Conference and the second best record in the league. Now, that was amazing for me to be on a team that ended the regular season with such great stats. We would meet Tampa Bay in the first round of the Stanley Cup Playoffs.

This was a first for me, playing in the NHL playoffs. Atlanta had never made the playoffs. I knew the Senators could beat Tampa Bay.

We played our first game at home. The crowd went crazy when we stepped onto the ice. I loved playing back in Canada because of the amazing fan base that we have. And I quickly learned that I loved playoff energy; it fired me up.

We won our first game, 4-1. Then we lost our second home game, 4-3. With the series tied, 1-1, we hit the road. We were off to play in Tampa for two games.

I knew my team had to win on the road to win the series. The Senators didn't just win one game; we won both games on the road. The first game was by a score of 8-4 and the second game was 5-2.

> *I loved playing back in Canada because of the amazing fan base that we have.*

Back in Ottawa for game five, our Sens fans cheered like crazy when we won, 3-2, in a nail-biter to win the series, 4-1. I was so glad my team won in just five games as it gave us a little more rest in between series.

The rest didn't do that much good, though. We ended up losing to Buffalo in the second round after just five games. In just ten playoff games, I managed to score three goals and get nine assists for a total of 12 points.

With the season over for another year, my determination bubbled quietly inside me. Next year my team would go further in the playoffs.

Now I had two more career goals to achieve. One was to win an Olympic gold medal and the second was to win the Stanley Cup.

◄ *Scoring my 50th goal for the Ottawa Senators in 2006.*

CHAPTER SEVEN

DOMINANT CANADA DANY HEATLEY

STANLEY CUP FINALS

When the 2006/07 NHL season started, the puck wasn't zooming past the goalie like it usually did for me. I tried everything to get that click going. Finally, around November, I started to find the open spots and the red light started to flash. It seemed like all of us started to click again and the Ottawa Senators became a team destined to do well.

For the second year in a row, I finished the regular season with 50 goals. This was a milestone because I became the only Senators player since the 1999/2000 season to do this. And I was only two points shy of Vincent Lecavalier's 52 goals. My points total came to 105 for the season and this broke the Ottawa Senator's record. I was fifth in the league in scoring.

I was thrilled when I was selected to the First NHL All-Star Team. At the All-Star game I was back playing with Daniel Briere whom I had played with in Bern, Switzerland. Hockey is like a big family and reunions with guys you used to play with are fantastic.

But I can honestly say that none of the excitement from any of those milestones or accomplishments were in my mind when my team, once again, made the playoffs. We were a team and; we were out to better our record by going further in the playoffs. We didn't finish on top in the regular season; instead were middle of the pack with a fourth place finish in the Eastern Conference. The Buffalo Sabres took top spot.

When the NHL season came to a close and the last game was played, we found out we were playing our first round against the Pittsburgh Penguins. I knew my team was better than the fourth place finish we had mustered for the regular season. I also knew that the Penguins had a really young team. I was convinced they could be beaten.

On April 11th, we played the first game of the series at home. In front of the home town crowd we easily beat the Penguins, 6-3. I scored the winning goal and I tell you that was a great,

◄ *Winding up for a shot. I think that's Marty Brodeur in net.*

great feeling. Then we lost our second game in the series, but that was the only loss. We ended up winning the series 4-1.

Last year my team hadn't gone past the second round so when it came time to play the New Jersey Devils, we got so fired up. We continually talked in the dressing room about how we could do this even though we knew the Devils were a strong team and were favoured to win the series.

That first game was on the road at the Continental Airlines Arena. Against the Devils' home crowd, we quickly jumped to a 4-0 lead in the first period. Can you believe that? We were on a roll. I scored the fourth goal and we went crazy.

We went to the dressing room full of energy but when we came back out the Devils had changed. They pressured us like crazy. It was such a hard game. The score ended up 5-4 for us but we knew we had been lucky. There was no way the Devils would let us have a lead like that again.

For the next game, we all prepared to play hard hockey.

Alfredsson had the only Senators goal in the first two periods. Late in the third period, the score was 2-1 for the Devils. My line was out. I couldn't let my linemate Aldfredsson do it alone so I charged down the ice and ripped the puck past Martin Broduer to tie the game.

That game went into overtime. The first overtime period was scoreless. It's so hard to play a lot of overtime periods in playoff hockey. The pace is so fast. At 1:55 in the second overtime, the Devils scored and the series was tied.

In the hotel room Chris and I talked. "We can win," Chris said.

"You got that right," I said.

We returned to Ottawa. I was confident that our team could win. In front of our home crowd we beat the Devils, 2-0! It was quite a game because both our goals were scored late in the third period and one was into an open net just after the Devils had pulled their goalie in an attempt to tie it up in the last minute of play. It hadn't been a cake-walk, though we certainly gave our fans a good show for the price of admission. The fourth game was the same and both teams were evenly matched but we came out in front 3-2. In that game I scored the second goal for the Senators.

Back in New Jersey, we wrapped up the series, winning 3-2. That was such a relief. We had won our second round and had gone further than we had the year before.

All the way home on the plane, we each thought about winning the next series. The Senators were on a roll. We were to either play the Buffalo Sabres or the New York Rangers. My team had been at odds with the Sabres all year. In February there had been a huge brawl because Chris Drury was knocked down by a hit from our tough guy, Chris Neil. The Sabres rushed to Drury's defence and then the game got out of hand. Since that game, every game against them had been heated and controversial. Even the coaches from the two teams didn't get along.

All the way home on the plane, we each thought about winning the next series.

When we heard the news that we were to play the Sabres, we got so excited. I knew it would be a good but tough series. We all did. What I didn't expect, however, was that we would handle the Sabres in just five games, taking the series 4-1. I thought for sure we'd go seven games. But it certainly wasn't a one-sided series as all the games were close. I scored just once in the series but our C.A.S.H. line managed to be leaders in scoring. My linemates were playing awesome.

Now we were headed to the Stanley Cup finals! I had dreamed of playing for the Stanley Cup since I was a little kid playing minor hockey. And every NHL player dreams of winning the Stanley Cup.

Unfortunately, my team wasn't prepared for the Anaheim Mighty Ducks. It was almost as if our steam had run out. It was a similar series to that against Buffalo where each of the games were close with victories decided by just one goal. Against Buffalo, we came out on top. Against Anaheim, however, we just couldn't come away with the wins. We lost, 3-2, in the first game and just 1-0 in the second game. Then we saw a spark in the third game and beat the Ducks, 5-3. But then we lost in the fourth game, 3-2. I scored in that game but it wasn't enough to lift the team to a win.

We headed into the fifth game knowing that we had dug ourselves into a massive hole. Anaheim dominated from the beginning of the game and won 6-2 to win the Stanley Cup in front of their hometown fans – which is always a thrill for the winning team. It was so sad to stand on the line and watch them skate around with the Cup. Losing is not fun. The fans in Anaheim were so excited, though. Jason Spezza, Daniel Alfredsson and I finished in a three-way tie for points in the playoffs. Alfredsson had 14 goals and 8 assists, and Jason and I each had 7 goals and 15 assists. It was good that we all shared the points record.

It was an amazing thrill to play for Lord Stanley's Cup, though definitely a disappointment to lose in the finals. But one day my team will win the Stanley Cup and I'll hoist that coveted silver trophy high above my head in pride. In the fall of 2007, I signed a new six-year contract extension with the Ottawa Senators.

I still have two big dreams. One is to win an Olympic Gold medal and the other is to win the Stanley Cup.

My playing career is far from finished.

Dominant Dany Heatley

I'm hoping to make the 2010 Olympic Team. This is from the 2006 Olympics.

DEDICATION

To my parents and my brother, Mark. You have always been there for me through thick and thin. You are the main reason why I am where I am today.

ACKNOWLEDGEMENTS

I would like to thank my parents, brother, all coaches, teammates in minor hockey, the Calgary Buffaloes Midget AAA team, teammates with the Calgary Canucks, teammates with Calgary Canucks, teammates with University of Wisconsin, teammates in Atlanta and teammates in Ottawa. I would also like to thank Hockey Canada, all the Team Canada's I played on, and to Lorna for helping me tell my hockey stories. It was an honour to have Wayne Gretzky provide the Foreword for this book, so my thanks goes to him for his kind words. And I also have to thank all my friends, especially Stacey McAlpine, and the rest of my family.

PHOTO CREDITS

Matthew Manor – Hockey Hall of Fame – Hockey Canada IIHF Images: p. 6, 9

Murray and Karin Heatley: p. 10, 13, 17, 18, 25

Hockey Canada – hockeycanada.ca:
p. 4, 20, 34, 38, 40, 46, 48, 50, 53, 56, 59, 65, 66, 68, 71, 79

McAlpine Sports Management: p. 28, 46, 60

McAlpine Sports Management, Getty Images and NHL Enterprises: p. 30, 45, 72, 74